Charcuterie of Thoughts

Charcuterie of Thoughts

Rathnakumar Raghunath

Charcuterie of Thoughts

First Printing, 2023
Reprint, 2025

rathnakumar@hotmail.co.in

The Stunning Owl – photo by Srikaanth Srinivasan
www.instagram.com/srikaanthsrinivasan

Illustrations:
Rathnakumar Raghunath and Reshma Dhanraj

Cover Design:
Reshma Dhanraj and Rathnakumar Raghunath

About the book

Charcuterie of Thoughts is Rathnakumar's highly anticipated sophomore collection of poetry.

Much like its previous iteration – *Smörgåsbord of Musings* – this book is a concoction made of love, life, laughter, anger, joy, despair, romance, disgust, yearning, pain, wonder, and hope. It's a tribute to the full spectrum of the human experience, with each poem offering a unique insight into the beauty and complexity of our existence, showcasing the richness of our shared humanity.

In essence, *Charcuterie of Thoughts* is a celebration of all that makes us human.

Note from the author

Dear reader,

Thank you for giving this little book a chance. I honestly can't believe you're reading this right now. It's been a little over a year since my last published work, and I was kind of beginning to wonder if I'd ever get this book out. I'm happy it's finally in your hands.

I wrote my previous book *Comeuppance* shortly after quitting a job that, toward the end, had become super toxic. I was on a break from work for the first time in 12 years and I can't tell you the sheer sense of joy and freedom I felt those first few weeks. My creative juices were flowing, and I was eager to create. I finished writing, editing, laying out the interior pages of the book and all that went with it, in a span of 10 days.

But with *Charcuterie of Thoughts*, it was a different story. I have to admit that this book took longer than I'd anticipated it, actually, scratch that, it took longer than I wanted it to take. It wasn't that inspiration didn't come to me or that I'd run out of the aforementioned creative juice. It was just the logistics of it all. I got a new job that's been very demanding and suffice it to say that weekends were when I could actually sit and type these poems out. Naturally, it took the time it did.

After *Smörgåsbord of Musings* did pretty well (to my utter surprise, if I may add), I started receiving several messages about wanting more poems, poems that reminded them of *Smörgåsbord of Musings*. And while horror is my favorite genre to read, I enjoy writing poetry the most; poetry in my style – simple and relatable. So, this felt like an absolute labor of love. It married my desire to write poems and the readers' choice of wanting a "sequel" to *Smörgåsbord of Musings* together. Like the French enthusiastically say, « C'est bien tombé ! » it fell into place nicely.

My favorite thing about *Smörgåsbord of Musings* was that you didn't always know from whose point of view a particular piece of text was written. My true goal in writing that book was to have the poetry resonate with you, the readers, in a way that it didn't really matter who was saying those lines. The perspective was subjective. And it's that very same approach that I took for this book too. After all, we're human and we all feel – both differently and, at a lot of times, shockingly similarly.

I truly hope that you find a friend in this book.

Lots of love and gratitude,
Rathnakumar Raghunath

P.S., in keeping with the tradition of the *Smörgåsbord of Musings* poems' having titles in the French language, Charcuterie of Thoughts, too, will have titles in French. Got to keep the inner Francophile alive and happy!

About the author

Rathnakumar Raghunath was born in 1988, in Chennai, India. While he was more inclined toward music as a child, as he grew older, he developed a passion for languages. In school, he wrote a couple of short stories and won the Camlin Young Author award for his work, "It Happened One Night: And It Changed My Life."

He claims that his life changed the moment he saw the French-Canadian singer, Céline Dion, perform on a show on TV back in 2003. He fell in love with her pure talent and her down-to-Earth personality, and he was inspired to pursue courses in the French language in order to understand her French repertoire. He has done C1 in French at Alliance Française de Madras and A2 in Spanish at Instituto Hispania. During college, he wrote and directed a couple of short films, one of which also won the Bimbam Award for Best Concept. He has, since, gone on to bag acting roles in various musicals and plays such as "Archie: The Musical," "Oscar," "Stay by My Side," "Skipping Christmas," "Star of Wonder," "Moulin Rouge," and has performed in Concerts such as, "Magic of Musicals 2," "September Symphony," "Magic of Music 3," where he opened the show with Michael Jackson's "Earth Song." He was also a part of a tribute to Simon and Garfunkel and performed with the Philharmonic Society of Selangor Choir from Malaysia. He also features in a Gospel album by Jere Franklin titled "Jeeva Raagangal." He was one of the singers in the single, "Kindle the Fire" that was an official entry in an international competition in 2013. He was the "Artist of the Week" on 104.8 Chennai Live FM in 2015. He is currently following a career involving the French language. He also is a budding entrepreneur and has an online handmade jewelry and gift shop called Something Different. During the COVID-19 Lockdown of 2020, he created an IGTV comedy series called "Rawrange Series." Through everything that he has been doing, his passion for writing has always stayed with him. It is that which has pushed him toward writing more short stories and modern poetry.

His first published work is "**Elevator**," a flash fiction that has won the Literally Story prize. It was published in 2019. His first book of modern poetry is "**Smörgåsbord of Musings**." It has sold over 2500 copies and has won The Author Pages 2021 award for Best Debut. He has also written a small collection of poetry in French called "**Les Cicatrices**," which was a #1 bestseller on Amazon. He has a series of e-books called Digital Pride. It is a series of LGBTQIA+ short stories that will be published every year in time for Pride Month. "**Catch Me 'Cause I'm Falling**" is the first story in that series. It became the official selection for NE8x Litfest 2021. "**Comeuppance"** is his 5th publication and first thriller/horror novelette. It has won The Author Pages 2022 award for Best Thriller, placed 2nd in the Indie Author Championship 2022, and won the Cinemura Award 2022 for best book to be adapted into a film or web series.

He is currently working on his next book. He also has plans of translating his work into French and Spanish. Audio book versions of his works are also under production.

He can be reached at:
rathnakumar@hotmail.co.in
www.facebook.com/Rathnakumar.Raghunath
www.instagram.com/SomethingDifferentStore

For my **parents**, **Chitra Karthick** and **Karthick Raghunath**.
For **Jere**, for **Noah**, for **Céline Dion**.

For my sisters, **Rupashree** and **Jacqueline**.

For **Lavina**, **Kevin, Yeshaswini**, **Aneesh**, **Aburvaa**, **Srini**,
Gabriella, **Makrand**, **Kanagapriya**, **Manoj**, **Priyanka**, and **Sarika**.

Contents

Rathna Kumar

Peut-être

Maybe
Right now
You, too, are thinking about me

L'amour et la rassurance

No one can show you so much love that you will never question its genuineness
No one can give you so much reassurance that you will never feel insecure about not getting enough of it
There are definitely going to be times when you don't entirely feel secure and need more love
And if you are with the right person
You will never feel uncomfortable to ask them for more of it

Personne d'autres

The trouble is
Nobody else does it for me

La bonne journée

Whatever is going on with your life right now
You're taking a moment to read a book
That must mean it's a good day after all

Le confinement total

I opened the door to my closet and took out my usual perfume
I hadn't even taken a shower yet, but I sprayed some onto my skin
The citrusy fragrance of bergamot filled my senses
Transporting me to many a memory of dressing up in fancy clothes and getting ready for date night

But the whole world is on lockdown now
And this was the closest thing I could do to mimic going out with you for real

La réponse

While texting, I'd rather have someone respond with a "K" than with that disgustingly impertinent "👍"

La fleur

I was never too vain, and you were never one to fall for outer beauty
But I always tried to look presentable when we'd met to spend time
I wanted to look good for you
I wanted to smell good for you
I didn't want my stubble to scratch you
I didn't want chapped lips when I kissed you
But after we said our goodbyes, I stopped caring about how I looked
I threw personal grooming in the dustbin along with the tissues that dried the last of my tears
For a minute I thought I was being stupid not to care about this stuff
But something told me you too were being exactly like I was
No elegant dresses, no make-up, nada
Because you always used to say
"What good is a flower that blooms
When there's no one to admire it?"

Savoir

My friends knew I was in love with you
Even before I knew I was in love with you

Chagriner

When my dad passed away
Everyone came to me and said
"You have to be strong for your mom."
"You can't break down; she won't be able to handle it."
And I'd understand and nod politely
I knew I had to hold the metaphorical fort
But what about my grief?
I needed to let it all out
It was my loss too

So, I would lock myself in my room and bawl like an infant
And when I could, I'd steal away moments to lean on my love's shoulder and cry
It is important do to so
All that pent-up sadness is not good
It will manifest itself later horribly

And now when I meet an unfortunate somebody who's lost a loved one
I tell them this
"You are not a robot
You have feelings and therefore
You need to grieve first"

Le tien/la tienne

I've been yours for as long as I can remember that I don't know how to be mine

Faner

We will perish one day
Only fake flowers don't wilt

La majorette

If I can't be your coach and guide you
I will at least be your biggest cheerleader

J'attendais

You said you had to finish college first
I waited
You had to get a job before you could make a commitment
I waited
You needed a promotion to ensure financial stability
I waited
You wanted a better job because you didn't want to settle for less
I waited
When it was almost finally about to be time for me
You started working on your next lie

La survie

I might look fragile
I might seem weak
But when faced with adversity
I will stand up and fight
I will brave the elements
I will weather the storm
I will survive

Ineffable

If you ask me why I dislike someone, I could give you a thousand reasons

If you ask me why I love someone, I don't think I could articulate clearly enough

L'aiguille

I gather the purest cotton from the harvest
I pick out the softest muslin from the market
I cut a piece of the finest string I could find
I close my eyes and picture you in all your glory
I take a pair of scissors and cut away at the cloth
turning it to mimic every contour of your face and
every curve of your body
I thread a needle and start to sew
I fill it with the cotton
I stitch more to secure every gap
It is ready
A you-shaped doll
Only a couple of things to do now
I sit down
Place *you* in front of me
I light the candles that surround us
I look at you
I take the now threadless needle in my hand
I say, "You will pay for not loving me."
With one swift motion
I plunge the needle
Into your heart
The candles blow out
I smell blood
I light a match

The you-doll is gone
Suddenly, I feel it
Pain
Excruciating pain
I look down
And there it is on the left side of my chest
The bloody needle

L'étranger

If you can be kind to a stranger
You can be kind to yourself

L'apathie

How can you say I mean the world to you
When you don't even have the time for a phone call with me?
How long are you going to dangle a carrot in front of my gullible self?
What if one day I wake up and stop believing your bullshit?
What if I put my foot down and realize
I'm worth all the love in the world and decide not to take crap from you anymore?
The moment I decide to live for my happiness
The moment I flip the switch
You will lose the hold you have on me
And believe you me, you do not want to be in that place where all I have for you is apathy

Le remède

You are the remedy
But you are the pain too
You rock the cradle
But you smother the baby with a pillow too
Why can't I have one without the other?
Why can't you just be benign?
Why can't you be the sweet nectar that the bees take?
Why can't you be the sweet honey that the bees make?

Les sons

There are pleasant sounds
The sound a cuckoo bird makes is one of them
The sound you hear as you type away on a keyboard
is satisfying
The sound you hear as you crack the crust on a
crème brûlée is comforting

Then there are unpleasant sounds
The sound of a loud foghorn early in the morning
when you're still asleep is enraging
The sound of off-pitch singing is downright
blasphemous

But there are those sounds that are unpleasant, yet
important beyond measure
The sound of a dog's bark when it spots an intruder
The sound of a baby's reassuring first cry
The sound of an ambulance as it speeds forth
clearing the way to save lives
All unpleasant, but unfathomably important

Les ailes

I ask not for you to be the wind beneath my wings
I simply ask that you not cut them
I simply ask that you not curb my freedom
I simply ask that you not cage me
For I am a bird that wishes to take flight
And return home only when I think it's time

L'obscurité

All I see is darkness
I've been inside the belly of the beast for hours now
Having nearly surrendered to my fate, I close my eyes
Because keeping them open doesn't serve any purpose
My eyes don't do what they are intended to do
I'm all alone in this pitch blackness, marinating in the beast's digestive juices
Shouldn't I have been dead by now?
When all is lost
How am I still breathing?
More importantly, why am I still breathing?
Am I waiting for someone to come save me?
Can anyone even pull me out of this obscurity?
Is there still a glimmer of hope within me?
I stay there and watch my breathing become more and more strained
I know there are people outside, I can hear them
They know I'm dying inside
I hear cries
I can hear them try
They are fighting the beast from outside
It's not going to be easy
The beast is gargantuan

They are not going to get through to me
It is over
I'm going to die
And just as I start to give up completely
I hear a voice from outside the beast
Though muffled, I can tell that it is familiar
It is you
"Don't give up! Fight! You can come out of this alive!
I need you! I love you!"
"I love you too," I say almost involuntarily
As my words resound in the hollow chambers of the colossal beast that is holding me captive
I realize that neither you nor anyone else can fight this beast for me
This is my battle
I have to fight it from the inside
I don't know what it is that comes over me
But I feel like I have the strength of a thousand elephants right now
That little flicker of hope has now been fanned into a flame by my love for you, by your love for me
A raging flame that can annihilate the beast from within
I bury my fingers, nails, and all, into the warm interior monster flesh
I claw at it
I do not stop

With all my might
With every ounce of my leftover strength
I tear open its stomach from inside
The first rays of light hit me as the beast screams in defeat
I jump out of it
I can breathe easily again
I am free
Now I know one thing for sure
No one could have fought this battle for me
No one could have saved me
I had to do it on my own
I had to find hope
I had to remember I have things worth living for
I fought knowing you were there to cheer me on
I won the battle
I rescued myself

Oui, toi

You
Yes, you
I only wish one thing for you
That you smile with all your heart
Without grief ever lurking behind those pearly whites

Les requins

We are two people who don't have to do much
For the world to see that we're in love with each other
We assume we can trick people into believing otherwise
In front of them, we act like "friends"
Which we also are, anyway
So, it should be easy to pull off
Or so we think
But love has a way of revealing itself in the most explicit manner
It will find the narrowest crevices of our being
And ooze out like blood from a cut vein
Dripping into the ocean, leaving its scent
For the sharks to circle in

En demi-vie

I woke up this morning feeling dreadful
With tears on my pillow
Feeling only half alive
All because you said you didn't love me anymore

Le bon Horcruxe

When an author writes a book
Especially his first
He pours his heart into it
It is more than just a collection of words
That have flown out from his mind
Contained within its pages
Is a piece of his soul
He essentially creates a Horcrux
A good Horcrux
A Horcrux that then finds itself
On the bookshelves of several different readers
Readers that, he hopes, will cherish and
Treasure that piece of his soul
And when that happens
He becomes immortal
Years might pass
His human body might perish
But as long as his book is being read
As long as it finds a home on bookshelves
And until the last one of those books is destroyed
He will continue to be alive

Le lit vide

After I returned home from having spent time with you
I entered my bedroom with a sense of familiar melancholy
I stared at my empty bed
My empty bed stared right back at me
I walked toward it and placed the little present you gave me on it
I got undressed; laid the clothes neatly next to the present
Clothes, which now had your scent along with mine
Next, it was my cellphone, whose internal memory was running out thanks to the messages from you and the pictures of you
I put it down near the edge of the bed
I then placed the sound of your laughter and the touch of your hand
Somewhere on the bed between the taste of your lips and movement of your hips
Followed by the placement of the joke I said to make you laugh like a mad person
And then, it was time for me to lay my longing for you right in the middle of the bed
And lay it, I did
I stopped and sighed

I took a few steps back to see the entirety of what was in front of me
Suddenly, my bed didn't seem so empty after all

Le tigre

I am a tiger
My scars are the stripes

La lune

The more I spent time with you, the more I saw your true colors
The façade you maintained for all those days slowly started getting replaced by the ugly truth
The longer I was with you, the more clearly did I understand that I was a fool
A fool for thinking you were the radiant moon
When all you were was its distant reflection in a deep, dark well

Le sushi

Maybe my love language is offering you
the last piece of sushi

Maybe your love language is
letting me have it anyway

La décision

Empty is one side of my bed
I've been crying, my eyes have turned red
A day ago, I'd turn my head and see you, sleeping right there
Now, there's only a pillow; on it, maybe a strand of your jet-black hair
Where was the heads-up? Why did you leave me out of the blue?
You should have told me you were unhappy, for I didn't have the slightest clue
No one can replace you, so I know what I have to do
I will kill myself and make the other side of the bed empty too

Faire mal

They say that love hurts
That's not true
The lack thereof does

Mon parcours

My path wasn't filled with a bed of roses
Hell, it wasn't even laid with jagged-edged stones
It was one of cracked pavements and broken roads
I don't want to romanticize the pain and struggle
I'm not going to sit here and tell you that it was necessary to go through the hardships so I can fully appreciate finally having reached a good place
No, I won't lie to you
It should have been a smoother route for me
I deserved an easier journey
But it was what it was
And so, I'll tell you this
Despite the fact that every waking minute was a nightmare
I learnt that I'd had it in me to keep going
I surprised myself with how much I could handle
So, I will tell you that you, too, are probably made of sterner stuff
You, too, are made to persevere
You, too, are made to surmount all the obstacles that life has in store for you
And ultimately come out the other side, a stronger person, a more mature person and definitely
A happier person

Dis-moi « Je t'aime »

Don't whisper "I love you" softly in my ear
Say it out loudly
Say it out fearlessly
I deserve it
We deserve it

J'écris

When I'm lonely
When I'm scared
When I'm vulnerable
I write

When I'm in pain
When I can't scream
When there is no one to hear me out
I write

But what I don't know is
If in the process
I am being healed with every word I write
or it is slowly killing me, one word at a time

Me perdre

I didn't get lost in your eyes
I found myself in them

Les fleurs

Give yourself time to heal
Flowers need time to bloom

La façon dont ils vous quittent

How someone breaks up with you
How someone lets you down
Will tell you everything you need to know about them

La larme

Let go, my dear, let go
Of the chagrin your heart does know
What good does hiding it do?
It is better to shed a tear or two
You will feel a weight lift off, this way
Believe me, my darling, when I say
That blessed are you for having cried
For what is a tear if not pain liquified?

Nos cœurs stupides

Our hearts have gotten so used to beating as one
That when we tell them to let each other go
They don't comprehend

We have to keep repeating ourselves
Saying we are two different people who need to go
our separate ways

Why won't our stupid hearts just believe us?

Les vagues

I'm convinced that the waves love the sand
Though they erase everything that is written on it
For though you erase all of my messages from your phone just so others won't find out about us
I'm still convinced that you love me

L'imbécile

I never craved pain
Until it was the only thing you could give me

La maturité

Sometimes, I think I'm a very mature person who is equipped to handle the curveballs life throws at me. But at other times, I look at the page number below and laugh.

Le courage

I see courage everywhere
I see it when the deer breaks itself free from the grip of the cheetah
I see it when the wildebeests chase away the lions
I see it when the mother bird takes her babies under her wings
I see it when princesses save themselves
I see it when immigrants speak in the tongue of their newly found home
But most of all, I see it in you
I see it when you have the chutzpah to say no to something you do not want to do
I see it when you choose to swim back up from the depths of your melancholy
I see it when you stand up to fight a bully
I see it especially when, despite having your heart broken before, you let yourself fall truly in love once more

Les diversions

Diversions are temporary panaceas

Les pâturages

Nothing is always exactly what is seems
The greenest of pastures could be hiding secretly
buried bodies underneath

Le prison

The way I'm feeling right now
I want to be locked in a prison cell
I know it will confine me
I know I will lose my freedom completely
I know I will be stuck inside till I die
But at least it will keep all the others out

L'attente

You're not brave enough to tell me it's over
I'm not brave enough to tell you we're done
We're both just hurting each other
Hoping one of us finally breaks down and ends it

L'espoir, c'est dangereux

If you don't love me back
Tell it to me right away
Don't be nice to me
Don't patronize me
You don't even have to let me down easily
Just be blunt about it
Tell it to my face that you don't feel the same way
Rip the band-aid off in one swift motion
Because the longer you take
The more hope you are giving me
And hope, my love, is a dangerous thing

Le baiser

The day you held my face in your hands
Asked me to close my eyes
And then proceeded to kiss my lips ever-so-softly
Was the day I started living

L'amour lunaire

What's happened to us?
Our love was like the waxing moon
Growing a bit every day
More and more prominently
Until it was full
And everyone could see how brightly we shone
But now, it has started to wane
And it will continue to
Until it is completely erased
From the skies of our hearts

Les poissons rouges

Maybe goldfish don't have poor memories at all
Maybe we tell ourselves they do to make ourselves
feel better about confining them to small tanks

Le goût de sang

You're not helping me by keeping quiet
Every word that doesn't leave your mouth
Secretly lusts for my blood
Your silence is just disguised violence

La leçon apprise

Thank you for teaching me that is possible to continue to live with immense pain

La permission

Go ahead
Color outside the lines

Le cœur brisé

May the pain wilt away
As a flower does after four days
May the memories fade away
As color photographs fade to grey
May time become
My only dependable friend
May he once and for all
Heal my broken heart in the end

Le conseil

I was in one of my – *Ugh, it's Sunday evening already. That means I have to go to work tomorrow. I don't feel like it!* – moods. I was ranting to my friend saying how I wished I didn't have to be stuck at this soul-sucking corporate job and instead have money automatically be deposited into my account every month so I could actually do the things I love. I would work on my fitness. I'd write books. I'd record music albums. I'd act in plays. I'd direct short films. I'd do so much. And you know what? I'd actually be relatively decent at some of them. I'd even find time to give back to the community.

The bubble was getting bigger and bigger as I kept adding one awesome thing after another to my catalog of things I'd do if I had that kind of money. I paused for a second. And, looking at my friend's poker face, I asked, "What should I do to make this happen?"

My friend, in her typical deadpan manner said, "Get a sugar daddy."

La destruction

What
many
don’t
tell
you
about
love
is
how
easily
it
can
destroy
you

La déclaration d'amour

The casual way in which I play with your hair
The adorable way in which you wipe the sweat off my brow
The way I look at you, in awe, even when you're doing the most mundane of things
The way you always hold my hand, almost involuntarily, whenever we cross the street
These little things speak volumes more about our true love
Than a loud, elaborate declaration of love in the middle of the street would

Le rêveur

I am a dreamer
Who would rather stay in his self-constructed dreamland than elsewhere
For when he is in the real world
He has to share you with everyone who vies for your love
In his dreams
You are all his
Only his

La poésie

I sat down to write poetry
I had to put something on the paper
I needed inspiration
So, I thought of you
I thought of you for a moment
I thought of you for a long time
And then I got up and walked away

I decided to leave the paper
Exactly the way you left me feeling inside

Empty

La plus forte personne

The strongest people in the world are those who are able to stay friends with someone they're in love with, knowing fully well their love will never be requited.

Le métro

When I sit inside the metro train
I keep looking at the previous compartments' movements
When I see that it slightly swerves to the right, I know a bend is coming
I know my compartment will follow suit and bend the same way

I want that in life too
I want to be able to see what's coming
I want to prepare myself for what's next
Life goes fast like a metro train
You never know what's going to happen
So, if you're planning on leaving me anytime soon
Tell me now
Bend a little, slow down your pace
Please give me a heads-up
If you're getting off the train at the next station

Ça me fait mal

Every morning I wake up, I hurt
I go to work, I hurt
I eat without enjoying the meal, I hurt
I return home, I hurt
The phone rings and your name flashes, I heal

La petite pause

Sometime in the middle of the night, I wake up wondering if my dog knows how much I love him. It pains me to know that I may never truly know what he desires. What if he wants to go see the world? What if he feels confined when he is at home with us? What if I'm not a good enough brother to him? So, I walk to the living room where he's sleeping, sit beside him and hug him as tears roll down my face. I tell him, "Know that you mean the world to me, and I will always love and protect you with every fiber of my being." And sure enough, he licks my tears away, making my face wetter than it was while I was crying.

Dear reader, if you're like me, do me a favor and go hug your dog now and then return to this book. You'll not regret the little break!

My sweet angel of a dog, Noah, passed away on the 12th of August 2021. I'd written this piece several months before that wretched day. He was my brother for 14 long years, yet somehow not long enough. He made me a better person and I did everything in my power to be there for him until he left this world to go to the Rainbow Bridge. I will meet him one day, and until then, I will find solace in the fact that Noah knew I loved him with all my heart.

La scène du film

A well-written movie scene
Beautifully performed by its actors with complete integrity
The expressions on their faces, sincere
The dialogue, powerful
But there was something missing
Music
The score came in and tied it all together
Elevated the entire scene and took it to the next level

My life was the movie scene
You were the music

Que ferais-tu ?

When you're in love, don't you want to just scream about it from the top of your lungs and tell everyone how much in love you are? Don't you want to tell every passerby how happy this love makes you?

But what if doing just that is enough to land you in trouble? What if anyone's knowing about it would result in your being judged? Judged badly, even. What then?

Would you bite your tongue and swallow your words? Or would you put on a brave front and let the world know that you're not afraid to love?

What would you do?

Le jeu toxique

What is this game you're playing?
Do you have the slightest idea I can play it too?
Maybe, I'd be better at it than you are
Did you think about that?
I sit here with the power in my hands to destroy you within minutes
Yet, I don't act on it
Why?
It would make me happy to have a win
I'd love all the support from the people around me
I'd finally make them all see the person you truly are on the inside
But why am I hesitating?
Is it because I don't want to stoop that low?
Is it because it's not in my nature to be cruel?
Or is it that I'm unsure you'd be able to survive the repercussions?
Is it that there is still a part of me, pathetic as it may be, that is still in love with the toxic you?

Le passé

Only the people who have nothing interesting going on in their present seem to dwell on their past

L'ami de mon enfance

I lost my husband
I was lonesome
I wanted a friend's shoulder to cry on
I picked up my phone to call you, my friend from childhood
I was not disappointed
You answered
You invited me home
We had a meal together
We spoke about several things
The weather, the city, our jobs
I noticed that you were careful not to bring him up
I knew talking about him would make me cry
But I also knew that you were there to comfort me
So, I spoke about the love of my life, my husband
I started to weep uncontrollably
You rushed to give me a hug
I leaned into your friendly warmth and let all the tears turn to dust
The moment I relinquished all control and became my most vulnerable self, I felt it
Your hand, grazing my back, slowly moving south
I'm imagining things, I thought
Your hands reached further down and squeezed me
I pulled away

What are you doing? I asked
Come on, I'm just trying to make you laugh, you said
What? How the heck is this going to make me laugh?
You pulled me towards you and started groping me all over
I tried to escape the clutches
I couldn't, you were stronger than me physically
I didn't scream, I was in shock
I kept crying through all the *Relax*es and the *Calm Downs*
I asked you to let me go
You said I'd enjoy it if I let myself
I don't want this, I said
I wanted a friend
You started yelling breathlessly
Don't act like you're not deprived of this
Who better to give it to you than a friend?
No one has to know about today
Deep down you know you want this too
Otherwise, you wouldn't have called me, he said
I couldn't believe what I was hearing, I thought
He was stepping on already broken pieces of my heart of glass
I trusted him
I came to his place because I'd always felt secure with him

I wanted to reminisce about old times and momentarily forget the pain of having lost the only man I loved
I didn't know he'd cause me more pain
He broke my trust
He betrayed me
The comfort of the 17-year-old friendship, gone in an instant
He was like a brother to me
How could he ruin this for us?
Was he always this way?
Were all the friendly hugs we had shared for all those years not entirely friendly?
Were they tainted by his perversion?
Was our entire friendship a lie?
Let me go! I plead
No! Trust me! You'll enjoy it
Give in to me
I knew I didn't have a choice but to do exactly that – give in
Okay, I whispered, still fighting tears
Okay! I promise I'll show you a good time
No! Let me, I said, as I knelt down in front of you
I looked up at you
You smiled and winked at me
I smiled back
I closed my fingers to make a fist

The two following sounds that pierced through the air came in quick succession
The first one sounded like a boxer punching a speed ball (although there was more than one here)
And the second sound was of a monster
A predator, screaming in excruciating pain
The entirety of which he totally deserved to be experiencing

Une vulnérabilité étrange

How is our love both a strange vulnerability and a quiet strength at the same time?

Le sang et les draps

How much more pain will this poor heart of mine take?
What will make it all go away?
Should I cut myself deeper than you metaphorically cut me?
Should I let the blood gush out of my veins and flow onto the sheets that soaked up our sweat for many nights and many days?

I don't want to die
I just want for the pain to end

How can you sleep at night
Knowing very well that I lie awake?
How is it okay for our true love to be dead
When the new love you're trying so hard to keep alive is nothing but fake?

L'éclat éternel de l'esprit immaculé

Sometimes I wish Lacuna, Inc. were real
I'd have scheduled an appointment with them the very day I lost you
You, the love of my life
I'd have had you removed from my memories
They'd have made a mental map of our entire love life
They'd have come over with their fancy equipment
They'd have done the *procedure*
I'd have slept peacefully listening to the whirring sounds of the wires connected to my head
Each of the memories of the times we'd shared
From the most recent one to the farthest one in the past
Would keep getting erased
One by one
The last time we kissed
The last time we made love
Our last fight
The last meal we had together
The first meal we had together
Our first fight
The first time we made love
The first time we kissed
All gone

All erased
All in one night
They'd be done with me
They'd pack up their equipment
Exit my house, making it look like they had never been there
The following morning, I'd wake up with no memory of you
All should technically be well
But would it really be?
I don't know
Because what we had was potent
Stronger than what most people have
What if it doesn't work?
What if I lose all our shared memories
But still know something was missing?

What if I'd still be living with a heart that doesn't know why it's broken?

(An ode to my favorite film of all time – one that makes me believe in love more strongly than ever – the brilliant Michel Gondry film: Eternal Sunshine of the Spotless Mind)

Les batailles quotidiennes

The mirror in front
Shows me a face that
Though jaded, is still calm
Thankful am I
For the mirror cannot reflect what is on the inside:
The ruins of the daily battles my mind fights against all that life throws at me

La persévérance

Come what may, I will persevere
I will not give up, I will not back down
I will turn every period into an ellipsis
Because my story isn't done
It will go on...

Pourquoi moi ?

I do not fear death
For I know
What comes after I die
Is exactly what came before I was born
Emptiness
When my time comes
I will walk into the light
The light that brought me into this world

I do fear death will come
Not for me
But for the ones I love
I do not know if I can let them go
The uncertainty of the when
The immediacy of the how
The excruciation of the thereafter
Dread becomes the norm
As I ask the all-important
Why them before me?

Le vrai amour

Love that gives birth to poetry is

True love

Il y a 14 ans

14 years ago, it was you
Today, it is still you
Decades later, it will continue to only be you

Avec toi, le déluge

You bring the flood with you
Time weaves a blanket to cover my wounds
And before I can start to heal, you come and unravel
its threads until there is nothing left to protect me
Avec toi, le déluge

Je te remercie

My love,
Thank you for choosing me over what's easy
Thank you for proving that our love is true

Le pouvoir de la relation

Someone once told me that the power of the relationship lay in the hands of the one who cared less. I disagreed initially. But time after time, I had been proven wrong. What people were saying was right. The power did lie with the one who cared the least. And I kept feeling like a loser for caring too much. But how does one balance this whole caring thing in relationships effectively? I was convinced there was no way to do it. I was sure that there was always going to be one person who cared slightly less about the other, and that person would be the one in control of the relationship. And the other one had no choice but to dance to the beat of the controller's drum. All relationships are doomed, I resolved.

But that idea changed when you came along. What was the difference this time around? That somehow, in a world of millions of people, two humans, who were capable of loving each other equally and acting upon it truthfully, had found each other. That's what it was.

With us, it was never about power
It was always about love

Nous tombons

From a pile of clumsy tiles
I was picked
I was taken away from the chaos and made to stand on the ground
I was ever-so-slightly skewed in different directions until I was placed perfectly in line with you, directly facing you
You weren't facing me, though
You were turned the other way
But I looked at you, standing there
Tall, and powerful like a superhero
I wanted you to turn around and see me too
But you never budged
And then suddenly, my balance was off
I lost control
I fell
I fell for you
I fell for you hard
And what do you know?
You lost equilibrium too
You became unstable too
You fell
You fell hard
Not for me though
But for the one in front of you

We’re dominoes
We have no way of turning around or defying gravity
So, we accept our inevitable heartbreaks
Hoping nature intervenes and pushes us toward each other so that we may have
A fighting chance at love

La révélation

You think you're so sly
You think I'm so gullible
You think I don't know the real you at all
So, you think you can con me into buying your façade
So, you lie to me
You think the truth will stay hidden
But don’t you know that lies can reveal to the
listener more than what the truth can?

La seconde vision

I usually watch a movie a second time only when I'm
super impressed by it and feel compelled to go again
I could love, love, love a movie and be completely
fine just watching it once at the movie theatre
I'd be contented
But, of late, I watch almost every movie at least
twice
Watching it once just doesn't give me the fulfilment I
used to get before
I feel like I've not even watched the film properly
Movies don't hit me the same way they used to
when we'd watch them together
Hand in hand
Laughing together
Crying together
Sharing popcorn
Sharing love

La durée de vie

We've made enough love to last us a lifetime
But the moment I see you
I want many more lifetimes

La lumière empruntée

When love deserted my island
I was left all alone
I looked up at the sky and there she was
Must be awfully lonely up there for the moon, I thought
But that didn't stop her from shining brightly, did it?
Her incandescence illuminated the entire island
I wandered around wondering if I needed anyone at all
Why can't I be my own moon?
Why can't I light up my own way and show myself which path to take?
I don't need anyone

And then it hit me
She is glowing with borrowed light herself
She needs the sun to be radiant
She needs the sun like I need love

L'après-midi

I'm sitting here on a rainy day wondering why time has slowed down
The heavy rainfall sounds like white noise on TV
I don't feel like getting a hot cup of tea and staring at the window, watching the streets get flooded
Instead, I prefer going back to bed so that I can momentarily forget this gloom that surrounds me
I try to close my eyes and drain out the sounds in vain
I don't want to watch anything on Netflix
I don't want to read books either
There's really only one thing that would turn the entire glumness around - calling you now
Talking to you, laughing at the jokes you make
I remember telling you:
Having you in my life is like having my own personal sun
When I'm with you, you brighten up even the darkest of nights
What do I do now that I don't have you anymore?
Could I still call you?
Wouldn't that be a selfish thing to do
When I know you want nothing to do with me?

Ugh, how I hate this rain!

Come to think of it, it's not just the rain
It's everything
The day, the night
The dark, the light
I dislike it all
A world where you aren't there to call me your
"Love"
Is no world at all
The Earth isn't my home anymore
Without you, I'm an alien

Vas-y

If you have to leave me
Leave me
I won't say no
But when you go
Could you please take our memories along with you?

Mériter

I wonder why I fell for the thorn when
The rose is what I deserved

Mes cauchemars

Why are all my nightmares of the same thing?
Why are they all of your deserting me?

Le sauveur

Was it when it pulled you out of the void?
Was it when it helped you grieve the loss of a loved one?
Was it when it motivated you to be the best version of yourself?
Was it when it became your only friend, making you feel less alone?
Was it when it helped you drown out the chaos around you to bring a smile to your face?
Was it when it became an integral part of all your celebrations?

When exactly was it that you knew that your savior had always been music?

Quizás

Maybe it is because I don't think myself worthy of being yours
That I write you love letters
In a language I don't speak

La télévision

I go about my day
Not paying attention to the deaths being reported
While my television gently weeps

There are cricket matches being played
Crowds cheering for their favorite teams
Still my television gently weeps

(COVID has been devastating. The second wave, even more so. We all knew someone that we lost to the disease. While there was a string of bad news, the economy was weakening too. Measures had to be taken to get things back to how they were. It was during one of those days, as the Beatles song, *While My Guitar Gently Weeps,* was playing in the background that this poem came to me.)

La bonne personne

When people tell me they haven't found the right one yet
I just tell them that they are lucky
For there is no one who can hurt us more than the right one can

La bouteille

I am a bottle in the ocean
I carry within me a message written specifically for someone special
But will that destined recipient ever find me?
I don't know
I have no control
The waves decide which way I go

La colère

You know what anger does to you? It makes you go crazy. Maybe that's why the American expression *to be mad* means what it does. Anger truly does blur the lines of what is sane and what isn't.

Think about this: When you are frustrated and red with rage over something your inconsiderate boss said, and you take that anger out on the keyboard as you try to log in to your work computer, does it usually let you in at the very first attempt? Does it not say *Incorrect Password*? *Try again*?

And then, you get angrier and retype the correct password with a fervor matched only by that of a blacksmith striking at hot iron. But still the screen shows *Incorrect Password*. You nearly scream, "What? I entered the right password! I know I did!" Your anger crescendos. You type again, furiously. *Incorrect Password* again. "No! It's not working."

You need to calm down. You take a deep breath. You try to relax. Your anger gradually starts to lose its grip on you. You get ready. You type each letter of the password, one by one. Softly – as if the keys were made of delicate glass that would crack at the slightest application of pressure. Slowly – as if you had all the time in the world. You press enter. The computer unlocks. Voilà! You are in. You let out a sigh. You can't help but feel a bit of shame for taking out your anger on an inanimate object. You also feel slightly embarrassed for having been outsmarted by said inanimate object.

But in truth, it's not the keyboard that flummoxed you. It was anger. It was your anger that made your brain think you were typing the right password, when in fact you weren't. It stopped you from seeing things as they were. It made you believe you were right when you couldn't have been, because if you were, you would have been granted access, would you have not?

That's what anger does to you. It fogs your brain. Just imagine you took a life-altering decision in such a state – a state oscillating between sanity and insanity. Disaster. It was only when you had actually let go of your anger that you were indeed able to type the password correctly and finally gain the entry – the entry that was denied to you earlier, not by the computer, but by your anger.

La tendence

When I flood your Instagram DMs with tons of pictures and videos of a brand-new food trend that I like, and you expertly Google restaurants in our city, and take me there the very same day, so that I'd get to enjoy that *trending* dish with you, I know that I am in the presence of love!

L'Oscar

Hey, I have a question.
Where did you put the Oscar you won for acting like you loved me?

C'est quoi ton excuse ?

Why did you get close to me if you knew you were going to hurt me eventually?

Akin to a tiger that crouches before pouncing on its prey, you hid your true self and waited for me to lower my guard down, so you could stab me right in the heart, when I was my most vulnerable self

The tiger has to do it for its survival

What's your excuse?

Vers l'avant

I will have to keep going forward
My life's car has no rear-view mirrors
There's simply no looking back

Ce soir

Tonight, the moon is full
But my heart is empty

T'as changé

Here you are, telling me that I'm not the man you had fallen in love with
Well, how can I be when I have been changing myself, little by little, every day in order to accommodate your needs?

L'haleine matinale

In the beginning, every morning, as soon as I'd wake up
The first thing I'd do is look at your beautiful, sleepy face, as you lay there next to me, and kiss you
You'd hate the morning breath, but you'd still kiss me back
I'd take advantage of the moment and try to slide my tongue in
You'd go, "Eww, not before we've brushed our teeth," and push me away laughing that adorable laughter of yours
I'd look at you and think I was the luckiest man on Earth

Now things aren't exactly the same
I still kiss you every morning
But you don't kiss me back
How could you, anyway?

Photographs can't kiss back

Cher poète

Dear poet,
When you see a person crying, what is the first thought that crosses your mind?
Do you want to console them?
Or do you want to find out what's making them cry?
And if you do find the source of the person's woes, what will you do?
Will you try to help them by doing whatever you can?
Or would you find their anguish "poetic"?
And, instead, listen to all you can from them, head back home, and write all about it?
Will their misery fuel your art?
"Inspire" your next poem?
When did it become okay to trade your compassion for your artistry?
Was it when you started calling yourself
A poet first
And a human last?

La mauvaise excuse

Poésie Poetry est
is la the mauvaise
poor excuse
excuse que that je
I me donne give
myself pour for
écrire writing sur
about toi you

Ton visage

It is enough for me to look at your face for one second to find ten thousand things I love about it

Tout de toi

Your parents say you and I are not a good fit
When I ask them why they would think such a thing
Their answer is that they know their daughter better than anyone, and that things won't work out between us in the long run
But when I protest and say you love me too, and you want to spend the rest of your life with me
They say no
They say I'm a fool for believing so
They say they know you
And that they know you don't love me
They are sure of it because they claim to know everything about you
But the truth is, they don't
They don't know you like I do
They don't know that I have seen you in ways no one else has
They don't know how your face looks when I make you come
They don't see the love in your eyes as you look into mine and scream my name out loud
They don't know the intensity with which you kiss me every time you say I love you
So no, they don't know everything about you

Le meilleur reste à venir

You have been hurt badly
Yet, you don't show the world just how much pain you are in
You go about your day working hard for the money that puts food on the table
You even spare a moment or two to help out a friend at work
You bring smiles to strangers' faces

But a great rage stems from within you
From suppressing the excruciating ache your heart has been feeling
Agony that your face has had to hide
But you don't take the anger out on an innocent person
That would be wrong, you think

You get home
You greet your family like nothing's wrong
You make small talk, and then you go to your room
Undress
Get into the bathroom
Turn on the shower
But even before the water can hit your tired body
Tears start running down your face

You cry
You let all the emotions out
You scream, but silently
You don't want to alarm anyone
And at that moment when the water from the shower becomes the hand that wipes away your tears, you stand there wondering if it's even worth it
This whole hiding-the-pain-business

Maybe you should deal with it differently
Maybe you, too, should go to a bar and get drunk
Maybe you should punch a wall
Destroy pieces of furniture
Maybe you should quit your job
And shrug the responsibility off

But you are not that person
You are better than that
You would rather take a brief break from reality
Cry your tears, grieve the loss, and get back to real life, than completely live in a land of delusion

You are a warrior
Though you lost the battle, you have to win the war
You have things to do
You have people that depend on you
But even if not for them

You have to live your life
You have to live it for yourself
The show must go on

There is so much more to life
You know it
You know you are stronger than you give yourself credit for
You know that though your heart is scorched, it is capable of love
It has so much more love to give
You deserve happiness
And you know, sooner or later it will come to you

So, you get out of the shower with more than just a cleansed body
You do so with a strong sense of self, clarity, and a teeny-tiny bit of hope

La raison de bonheur

When I say you're the reason for my happiness
I hope that it doesn't put added pressure on you
You don't have to be a certain way for me to
appreciate you
You be you
You do you

Le sport

I don't care for sports
But I'll come watch a match with you
Only because, when a player scores, and the crowd goes berserk, I can use it as an excuse to hug you tight in public

That's the only way two men hugging won't get judgmental stares

(Dedicated to my friend, Erica. She knows why.)

Un peu de gentillesse

When I was morbidly obese, I did not care about how I looked
Having said that, I never once looked at myself in the mirror and thought I was ugly
But after a dramatic weight loss
After looking at my reflection along the way and saying, “Not bad”
Things are slightly different now

My eyes have become more critical
Unforgiving even, at times
They scrutinize my reflection to find the teeniest bit of flab
The most meagre weight gain due to the pandemic lockdown is met with a hatred so strong
I find myself thinking I'm unattractive
I find myself grotesque
I fear I have body dysmorphia

But will this make me follow a stricter regimen?
Will this hatred fuel the flame?
It just might
But I don't think it would last very long
The hatred was soon turn into giving up
I will eventually give up

But if I start to look at myself with kinder eyes and choose love
And tell myself that I love this body enough to keep it in the best of health
Maybe, just maybe I will work on losing the fat more efficiently
And I will lose the weight little by little
Because love always trumps hatred

Mon parfum préféré

The day I'll have found my favorite perfume would be the day they will have made one that smells like my favorite book

L’éthique professionnelle

I’m constantly in awe of the work ethic of the human heart
It keeps beating though it’s broken

La bibliothèque

You know there is a book on your bookshelf that is
waiting for a long time to be read
Before you had it, you desperately wanted to get
your hands on it
You did everything you could to make that happen
And finally, when the book did come to you,
You lost interest
You got comfortable
You got complacent
You knew it was yours
You knew it wasn't going anywhere
It lost its value

How unfortunate for me
That in the bookshelf of our love
I am that book

La soif

Your presence brings about a thirst in me that all the water bodies of the Earth combined still cannot quench

Les anniversaires

Birthdays are special. I have always loved them. And look forward to it every year. It is *my* day, and the week leading up to it is even more exciting than waiting for Christmas.

Back when I was 8 years old, my parents and I moved to a new house. I found out that one of the neighbor kids had the same birthday as mine. I was not happy. I feared that he'd steal my thunder. I was quite upset.

All that pettiness changed when I found out that my mother didn't even know when her birthday was. My grandmother hadn't made a note, apparently. That saddened me even more. I asked Mom how she dealt with it. Then, she said that she and her mother, after several lengthy deliberations, decided that her birthday would be on Deepavali every year.

I sat there, transfixed, a kid, moved to tears learning that his mother, when given the choice to pick her birthday, instead of choosing a random day or a calculated date where no birthdays of the people she knew fell, chose a day knowing that when she celebrated it, the entire country would celebrate along with her. She didn’t find happiness in hogging the limelight, instead chose to share it with the world. And that hit me. There I was making a fuss about sharing my birthday with one friend, and there she was, happy to partake in the collective joy of the people around her. Mom taught me a lesson without teaching me one.

Écrire

When I'm sad
When my tears are falling on the paper
Displacing the ink and smudging the words
I write better

Les pluies de mousson

Dark clouds
As heavy as my heart
Are letting go of their pain
In the form of rain

People on the streets
As swiftly as they can
Are running away from the needles and pins
That are the raindrops piercing their skins

Buildings and houses
As unmoving as always
Are starting to seem blurry, as if seen through a block of ice
While my tears mimic the rain, my beautiful Chennai dissolves in front of my eyes

Les photos que tu prends

If I'm smiling with my eyes
Chances are, you're taking the picture

L'idiot égoïste

Only a self-centered idiot will expect the world to stop spinning because he is not ready to seize the day

Moi, saignant(e)

You cut me open
You sucked me dry
You tasted my blood
You made me cry
When you were done
You left me to die
Please tell me you loved me
At least just lie

Le caillou

You want me to keep my feelings hidden from the world
But my love for you spans oceans wide
And my heart is but a tiny pebble on a beach
How can it hold all this love inside?

La douleur exquise

You said you loved pain

I didn't know you meant you loved inflicting it

Le temps qu'il a fallu

Falling in love with you

F o r g e t t i n g   y o u

Le son des mots

Some words, when spoken out loud, go hand-in-hand with their meaning

Brute, for example, sounds harsh
While *Mousse* does have a soft-sounding quality to it
Then, there is a list of onomatopoeia
Boom sounds like an explosion
Hiss does sound like a snake

But there are other words that sound nothing like what they mean
And my favorite one of them is *Kerfuffle*

Kerfuffle sounds less like a commotion and more like a fluffy, adorable creature from Hogwarts

Le bagage

Your
partner
should
help
carry
your
emotional
baggage,
not
add
to
it

L'art

The only way she knew how to deal with her broken heart was to turn it in to art

Le patriarche

He was angry that you were not afraid of him
He wasn't used to anyone who would fight back
He was mad at you for being so alive
He was shell-shocked by your resilience
He wasn't sure he'd get away with it this time
He was beginning to get scared
He was going to have to behave himself
He was ready to apologize

Les insecurités

I woke up this morning feeling dreadful
With tears on my pillow, feeling only half alive
It wasn't difficult to remember what my horrible dream was about
It wasn't something I'd forget that easily
You said you didn't love me any longer
You didn't want anything to do with me anymore
That's it
That was the nightmare

It got me thinking whether it was a premonition
Were you going to leave me soon?
Was that what I was able to foresee?
After some pondering, I got the answer
It was a resounding *No!*
I wasn't a bloody psychic
I didn't become a clairvoyant overnight
It was a dream, a bad one, yes, but still only a dream

I didn't need to do anything to make you stay with me, because you weren't going anywhere
The only thing I could discern for sure, was that the dream was my insecurities being protected back at me

How insecure must I have been to conjure up something like that?
I should realize I'm worth it
I deserve you, just like you deserve me
I need to believe that
Not as easy as it sounds
This will take time
I will talk to you
I'll work on it
With our love, I will get more and more secure
And one night, when I go to sleep in your arms, I'll dream a dream that won't be a nightmare

Le sacrifice

Love doesn't mean sacrifice
If you're the only one doing it

L'ex

Now that we're over
My friends think I have a sickness
Every time I go and *stalk* you on social media
They think I do it to see if you're still hung up on me
or if you've moved on
They don't understand that I do it because it's the
only way I know you're okay

La nature

I saw something I shouldn't have
I saw you both kissing
The lips you were kissing should have been mine
But I didn't have the will to confront you
I felt nauseated
I was numb
I wanted to walk away
And as I did so, I looked like nothing had happened
My stoic face showed no signs of experiencing betrayal
But then the warm Chennai weather began to change
The sun disappeared all too quickly behind clouds darker than night
They looked heavy, like my heart, about to burst any minute
The winds got wilder
The trees swayed with reckless abandon
Leaves and twigs, falling to the ground from all sides
The traffic stopped
The motorists knew it was unsafe to drive their vehicles
Motorcyclists started gathering under canopies seeking shelter
There I was, braving the weather, walking in the

middle of the road, my clothes aflutter, disheveled
I must have looked deranged
People were calling out to me
Asking me to be careful
Right then, a tree branch fell just as I walked past it
Nothing deterred me, for there was already a storm brewing inside of me
I was alone
No one knew how I felt, no one could–
No, that's not true
Nature did
She expressed exactly what I was feeling
She manifested what was within me
The moment when I realized Mother Nature stood with me in solidarity, I got chills
I was moved to tears
And surely enough, the clouds, too, let go of the water they were hoarding
The gray road became freckled with dark polka dots
And within seconds, the entire road was flooded
It was mostly the rain that did it
But who's to say it wasn't my tears as well?

Tes silences

I paid attention to every word that left your mouth

If only I were smart enough to understand what your silences said too

La jalousie radioactive

Wildly jealous am I of the fabric that touches your velvet skin
Of the comb that runs freely through your luscious hair
Of the beads of sweat that run down your neck
Of the water that touches your lips

But all you're jealous of is how quickly *he* could break your heart, and go find another woman while you're left behind, pining for a love that died in his heart

Une journée au soleil

These past few days haven't exactly been easy
You have been working hard
You are just about exhausted, physically, and mentally
You've been secretly waiting for a day in the sun
And I'll tell you what, it will come sooner than you expect it
Here's to a guilt-free time off from all the hard work you've been doing, so you can spend quality time the way you choose to

Pourrais-je ?

I know you'll be there when I need you
I know you will give me a shoulder to cry on
I know I can come to you when my heart is heavy

But can I choose not to?
May I just heal in silence?
Most times, for me, talking about it doesn't help
I'm only reliving the trauma

Would you still be okay if I made my peace with it
before I talked to you about it?

Les uns et les autres

There are those who know what it is like...

- To be called a "fatso."
- To be almost always wrongly accused of being overeaters.
- To be scared of kids because they don't have a filter. They could look at you, in a crowded place, or a random bookstore and point at you and laugh, call their friends, and tell them how fat you look.
- To be the last names called out while choosing sides for sports teams.
- To be afraid of going to the swimming pool. Worried about what the bathing suit looks like on you.
- Not to be able to walk into just about any clothing store and find even one piece of clothing in their size.
- To be assumed to be older than they are just because they are bigger.
- To be presumed to be pregnant because their belly jets out.
- To have complete strangers ask questions like, "Do you really think you should be eating that piece of fried chicken?"

- To be told expressly that they'd look good if only they lost weight.
- To get used to not seeing leading men and women looking like they do on screen.
- To be compared to an elephant only because of its size.
- To be nothing more than a fetish.

...And then, there are those who don't.

De l'eau sous le pont

Can't we be friends now?
It's been a long time since we broke up
It's all water under the bridge

Of course, it is
Water under the bridge
That once nearly drowned me

Les cicatrices des moqueries

What is it about some relationships that turns toxic all too quickly?
You were my biggest cheerleader
But now all you do is find something mean to say every chance you get
I understand that those mocking words come from no place of malice
I understand that these are games that you play
because you never got to play them with others
But what about the indelible mark that your jibes leave?
Should I continue to act like they don't affect me?
You don't have to shower me with praises
But every time I do something that I'm happy with
Do you have to attack me with your piquant wit?
I've never been one to show off my achievements
I have never tooted my own horn
Then you came along and celebrated everything I did
Now, I'm scared to do anything at all
You made me get used to kindness from you
When did it change to vileness?
Once upon a time, you saw my baby steps as giant leaps
But now you make me feel like I don't have legs

L'aventure

Every time you kiss me
I embark upon a new adventure
That I never want to end

Notre histoire

I don't know if years from now
Historians will write about our love
But I'll die in peace knowing
I've filled some of these pages
With our story

Les chansons tristes

Sometimes,
sad
songs
do
what
even
therapists
cannot

Apprends-moi

Teach me how to share my love with all
Tell me how you are able to when I am not
You know I have a big heart
Capable of feeling a lot
But when it comes to showing it
Why am I not able to?
Why is my emotional bandwidth so small?
Is it because I am afraid of vulnerability
Terrified of getting hurt, of feeling too much?
Or am I simply unsure of how to express
The love that I hold within me?
Teach me your love language
I will be your student
Show me how to open my heart
And share all the love I have to offer the world
For when all's said and done
Isn't it the love that we give
That comes back to us?

Elle

Smile, she does a lot
Words, she only says a few
But that is all it takes to melt a frozen heart
And make it beat anew

La pomme pourrie

You are the oxygen in the air
You are good for people
You make them thrive
But for me, you are no good
You make my soul go dark
You turn me rotten
From the inside out
I am no people
I am a half-eaten apple

Le vol inutile

If you stole my money
And looted my gold
I will still be rich
For you can't steal that which is unstealable
The wealth of my knowledge
It will stay
Right where it always will
Within me
You know I will use it well
And earn back all that I have lost
So, you Machiavellianly take my clothes away instead
As you think it will embarrass me
You think it will shame me to no end
You think I will hide away for good
What a fool you are to think that way
For there is more enterprise in walking naked,
anyway

(An ode to the incomparable William Butler Yeats)

Les chefs

Is it just me, or does it make complete sense that, in gaming, the most horrible villains are called bosses?

Rupa

I confided in my little sister
Poured out my heart and soul
Admitting to feeling like a loser
A loser in love, with no control

The world was against
The love in my heart
It tried its best
To tear my love and me apart

I wallowed in self-pity
Sinking deep in profound sadness
When my sister, wise and witty,
Uttered words that brought me gladness

Her words linger in my mind
A reminder for many tomorrows
Of how a little wisdom can bind
Life's broken pieces and ease our sorrows

"How can you be a loser," she said,
"When you're still fighting for your love?
You're not giving up, you're not dead,
You're brave and strong, an eagle soaring above."

Her words rang true, I felt the flame
Of hope ignite within me
A warrior for love, I became
I'll win this war, you'll see

But it's not easy to fight
A societal enemy so strong
There are days when my love and I feel slight
And everything seems to go wrong

But when we remember her words
We'll find the strength to carry on
We'll rise like the phoenix birds
And sing our love's sweetest song

This, I want you to remember
So, I'll give it to you in writing
How can you be a loser,
When you're still fighting?

L’amitié

Friends come in all shapes, sizes, colors, genders, sexualities, ethnicities, and religious beliefs. Your job is to love and accept them the way they are. If you feel the friendship isn't enriching your life, it's better to walk away from it than to try and change the friend into someone they are not.

La vengeance

The news of your having chosen someone else over me found its way home
Immediately the desire to avenge surged through my veins
But when I realized you'd never get to taste the hunger on my lips again
Revenge turned into pity

Le baiser de minuit

No one believes me when I say that you love me
They laugh at me when I say that
you have kissed me
Though the kiss was at
midnight
In the middle of a
deserted street
I knew there was a
witness who could
testify for me
I flew to the moon
and asked her,
"What did you see?"
She said, "Alas, I saw
nothing,
For I was hiding behind a giant oak tree."

Ton temps

If you say you love me, choose me

Don't just give me bits of your time where I don't get enough of you

Getting some of you hurts more than getting none of you

Le scorpion

Whenever you see that I'm happy
You have a sick way of bringing me down

By now, it shouldn't even surprise me
It's in your nature to do so
And you can't change it

How can I begrudge a scorpion for wanting to sting?

Les faux admirateurs

One of the worst sorts of people in the world are the ones who find something you love and try to one-up you and make it seem like they love it the most.

There is definitely enough love to go all around, yes. It *is* possible for more than one person to love something equally or more.

But all of this applies only when their love is genuine.

Le lac

When you look at your reflection

in the still water of the lake

Did you know that it

counts you as

a second

moon

?

De la même façon

Here's the thing:

Sometimes, it all boils down to the fact of whether they absolutely love you or not.

You could love them with all your heart, but if they don't love you back the same way, you are always going to end up being disappointed.

La fausse inspiration

Being inspired by someone and copying from
someone are two different things
Inspiration is flattering
Copying is disgusting

Le confort

No matter how hard I try, I know that with you, I'm always going to feel inadequate. Even though I know that deep down you truly do love me, you're not going to do anything about it. You are always going to choose the comfort of keeping your parents happy over doing what's right to keep our love alive.

But who am I to lecture you on complacency, anyway? I'm a hypocrite, myself for choosing to stay with you knowing all this fully well, when I should have stepped outside the comfort zone of our love and ended things with you.

Instead of being loveless, I chose to be loved less.

Le chien divin

God forgives

Dog sevigrof

Le dîner

What are you having for dinner?

Memories of us.

So, you're okay with having your
dinner taste bittersweet?

Les mots qui tuent

If they said *actions speak louder than words*
I'm sure they didn't mean it in the context of
inflicting pain
For bruises from being punched get cured
Black eyes eventually disappear
But only very rarely do wounds caused by toxic
tongues and their noxious words heal

Savoir quand il faut s'arrêter

I've never been one to give up
Even after being knocked down several times
I've always had fight left in me still
But there have come times when I've had to decide if the fight was even worth it
It's okay to take a step back
It's not giving up if you know it's a lost cause
You're just being smart and saving your energy
Redirecting your efforts toward a more fruitful path

La seule raison

The
Only
Reason
You
Love
Me
More
Is
So
You
Can
Hurt
Me
More

La famille

You don't have to share genetic material to be family
It's enough if you share love

La ligne rouge

There is only so much pain I can endure
Keep hurting me the way you are and
One day my "I will die for you"
Will become "You're dead to me"

Les perspectifs

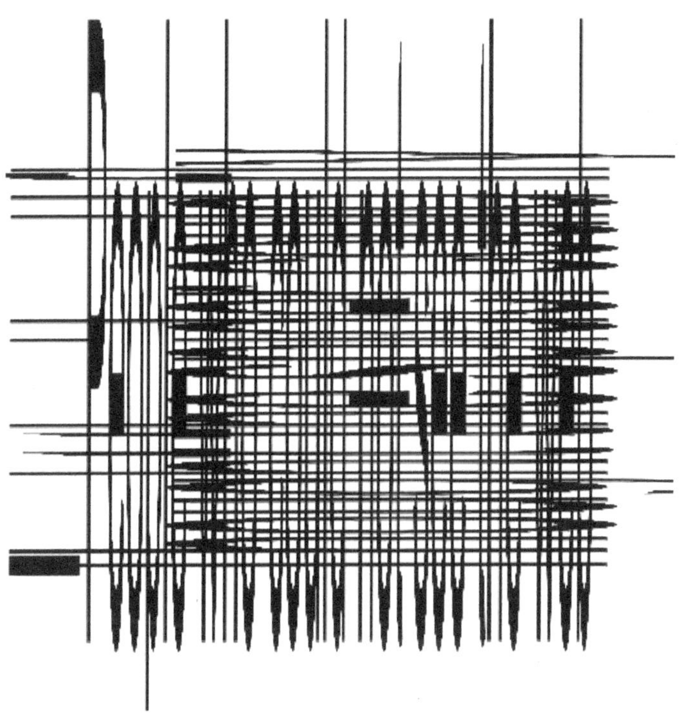

Chère femme

Woman, find your dignity
Don't let your man strip it away
You don't need to bend over backwards to prove your worth
It shines through when you're true to yourself
No need for false flourishes
No need for embellishments
Just by being who you are
Your transcendence never fails to reveal itself

Woman, find your self-esteem
You carry his burden along with your own
Shouldn't he help you with yours?
Don't let him walk all over you
Stand up for yourself
Fight back
He needs to give you the respect you merit
You deserve to smile with your heart

Woman, find your courage
You don't *have* to stay here
You've given him several chances
You've sacrificed a lot
Love shouldn't have to be one-sided
Leave, if it's the best for you

You're accountable only to yourself
No one has the power to stop you

Woman, find your freedom
Break the chains he's put around you
Take the keys and unlock the gates
To the glorified prison he calls your home
Step out
Walk
Run
Choose liberty
Choose happiness

L'amour pur

One
of
the
purest
forms
of
love
is
what
fans
have
for
their
favorite
artists

Le goût

Food tastes better
when I eat it
with you

Le réconfort du froid

I am fine
The bitter cold is my friend
The chilly air lifts me up
The snowflakes embrace me like long-lost family members
The lakes are frozen along with my heart
The cold blood pumps at the speed of a glacier
I am comforted by my chapped lips
When winter comes, I feel truly at home

But then you show up here with the intensity of a million scorching suns
Melting away the ice caps that guard my very soul
Go away and leave me to my icy ways, for I know
If you stay any longer, I will warm up to you
I will lose the winter, you will become my home
Will you be ready for that?
Or will you abandon me?

No, I won't take that chance
I won't let you melt me
So what if I don't have you to love?
The bitter cold is my friend
I am fine

Les roses sont mortes

Roses are dead
Violets are too
Everything has expired
Including my love for you

Le maître

I've lost all control over my body
There is someone inside my brain
He is pulling all the strings
He is my master
I am his puppet
He makes me do things I don't like
He makes me kill my will to live
He makes me want to die

What good is my body if my mind is broken?
I shudder to think of all the things I've left unspoken
If he continues to own me
I will become everything I hate
But what scares me more is that I will lose you

I want to break free
I have to sever these strings
But how do I do that when I can't even move a muscle?

I want him gone
But you know I can't put up a fight
I need you to come here
Please bring your light
I'll be the host

You be my parasite
Bore into my brain
Scorch me till he's slain

And in the process if I die
Then know that I loved you
But if I do survive
If I do make it out alive
Then know that it is only by
The miracle of your love

L'auto-réflexion

Sometimes, amidst all the chaos around me
I have to stop and take a look
Look at myself
As if I were another person
Look at myself
Check myself
Am I in the wrong?
Did I do the right thing?
Should I make some changes?
And when I am done self-reflecting
I start healing

Comme la lune

We are all like the moon
Always hiding a part of ourselves away from view
Never revealing whom we really are

Les animaux nocturnes

Though we love the light
We are forced to evade it
We run toward the dark
We seek out shadows
Just so we can finally be
Whom we truly crave to be:
Lovers

We are nocturnal animals
Not by nature
But by choice

Rien à prouver

Don't live your life trying to prove your childhood bully wrong

They're not worth it

Le saut de la foi

I lie down, staring at the blank canvas of the ceiling
Projecting onto it everything that is on my mind
All that I see are pictures of the two of us, feeling
Like we're the best person each other could find

Pictures of our kissing faces
Of our intertwined hands
Of our shared embraces
And of the uncharted lands

But as the minutes tick by, the pictures fade away
And the elephant in the room becomes harder to ignore
It's the unanswered questions that haunt me every day
About where we're heading, about what we're fighting for

So, I sit up, take a deep breath, and say your name
I clear my head, I'm finally awake
It's time to put an end to this senseless game
And take a leap of faith for our true love's sake

Le jardin

You tended to all the flowers in your garden
And amidst them, I blossomed too
Each day, you plucked a new bloom
I watched as they dwindled in number
Yet, my time never came, and I wondered why
Was my beauty not enough?
Did my fragrance not permeate?
Where did I go wrong?
But then it dawned on me:
You never picked me because I was the one
The one you loved the most
The one you couldn't bear to let go

Tout ce que j'ai écrit sur toi

Everything that I have written about you here
Has already been shown to me by you
By the kisses you have given me
By the love you have showered on me
By the strength you have accorded me
By the pain you have caused me

Rathna Kumar

Acknowledgements

My friends and I have this running joke about how the acknowledgement section of my books is annoyingly long. I can't help it. I just have way too many people to thank. It's important for me to be grateful, recognize, and give credit where it's due.

My mother is the reason I'm able to do this. I can't thank her enough for letting me put my mental health first, helping me in every way she can. I wish one day to be able to translate my work in Telugu so she can read and enjoy it. But for now, I'll tell her this: అమ్మ, నాకు అన్ని విధాలుగా మద్దతు ఇస్తున్నందుకు ధన్యవాదాలు. మీ పూర్ణ హృదయంతో నన్ను ప్రేమిస్తున్నందుకు ధన్యవాదాలు. నా గురించి గర్విస్తున్నందుకు ధన్యవాదాలు. నాన్న కూడా నా గురించి గర్విస్తారని ఆశిస్తున్నాను. మీ ప్రేమ ఈ పుస్తకాన్ని సాధ్యం చేసింది. నేను మీ దయ మరియు ప్రేమను ఎప్పటికీ తీర్చుకోలేను, కానీ నా జీవితమంతా అలా చేయడానికి ప్రయత్నిస్తాను.

Jere, thank you for being my biggest cheerleader. Thank you for directing the Comeuppance audiobook with such élan. I'm extremely proud of you for adding another feather to your professional cap. On a personal level, thank you for all your words that have healed me every time that life had pulled me down. I stand tall thanks to you. Thank you for making me believe in myself, and my craft. Most importantly, thank you for taking care of my heart. Je t'aime.

Céline, you're present in every good thing that I do. You're my life. Je t'aimerai jusqu'à la fin de ma vie.

Noah, mon amour doré, you continue to live within all of us. I love you more than I will ever be able to say. I miss kissing your golden face every day. I couldn't have asked for a better brother than you. I thank you for enriching my life and teaching me life's most important lessons.

Reshma Dhanraj, my books will be incomplete without you, pretty much like my life would also be. Thank you for being the non-toxic, no-nonsense, sanity-bringing friend that I believe I deserve. Love you loads.

Sarika, try as I may, but I'll never be able to thank you enough for all that you've done for me. You needn't have done half the things you've done to support me. But you've happily done them and continue to, as well. I for one am extremely lucky to have you in my life and I hope one day I can repay your kindness. Thank you for thinking of me as an author worth his salt.

Kevin, my dear Kevsy, thank you for being there before anyone else even gets slightly excited about any book I put out. Thank you for sharing your talent with me. Thank you for being my hype man. Ich liebe dich.

I want to thank all my friends who came for the book launch of Comeuppance. You didn't have to, but you did. You made me feel like a star that evening. Thank you. Thank you, Padmini, Dhiyanathiru (Brioche), Prashanth, Abhi, Sneh, Vignesh,

Naveen, Aparna, Porches, MiKe bro, Jo, Nivin, Renuka Akka, Karpagam, Maha, and my sweet, sweet Bagavathi Anna.

I want to thank my dear friend Makrand for helping me come up with the name for this book. I was talking about what a smörgåsbord was and he suddenly went, "Oh, like a charcuterie board?" And a light bulb came on!

Apart from the lifelines at work, Rupashree and Jacqueline, who take care of me like I'm their priority, I also have a bunch of incredible people who brighten up my work day, whom I have to thank for helping me stay sane – Simran, Joshua, Syed, Ashwin, Medha, Vignesh, Sathya, Neha, Gajalakshmi, Annie, Shwetha, Madhu, Akshay, Henna, Dwarak, Zaid, Namita, Rachel, Sanjana, Poovanna, Priya, Trisha, Farhan, Dev, and many others.

There are people in my life that I will always cherish, so many more friends I have to thank for supporting me through my journey as an author. Some of them are Swati Pal, Sherji, Natalie akka, Asma, Pavithra akka, Shrutee, Abi, Abhishek, Erica, Ashley, Lalrin, Divya, Chandni, Gaurav Srinivasan, Jaya Sakthi, GR Naveen, Harish, Ishika, Hemadharshini, Akshiv, Aathira, Jasmine, John Suhaan Appasamy, Joselin, Jo, Vishal, Charu, Kajol Srinivasan, Mushkan, Subin, Ruthran, Mansi, James Cobb, Mahadheer, Neeraj, Niru, Nissi Chrisolite, Priyanka Katrela, Rabhinder, Anupa, Revathy, Saikumar, Sakthi, Timothy, Srivarthini, Vibha, Shashwat, Soundharya, Megha, Coralie, Tridev, Meenakshi, Priya, Vasanth, and MANY more.

I would like to thank my students and brothers and sisters for enriching my life, my author brother Poopesh, Aneesh, Shyam, Harsha, Varun, Srini, Dinesh, Roshan, Prethe, Rahul, Naren,

Vyshali, Karan, Danush, KP, Chitra, Abi, Thameem, Sandeep, Karthi, Jenolin, Manoj, and more.

My readers whom I've become such good friends with – Garvy, Harsh, Vijaya, Aditya, Kajal, and Vanshika. My author friends – Vijaya, MathiRaj, Surya Sree, Akshath, Vibhuti, and more.

Shanaya Stephens, I'll eternally be grateful to you. Big hugs.

Srikaanth Srinivasan, for sharing his gift with me. Thank you.

I also want to thank everyone who has taken the time to review my work. A special thanks to Rachel from The Shades of Orange and Shree Janani. And Sharanya Kannan, thank you for existing!

I found a few people through my love of their work and their appreciation of mine, and I'll never be able to thank them enough for the love and support they've extended to me. Nakkhul, thank you for your kindness. Vayu bro, you are the best. Kalesh Ramanand bro, you know how much I love you. Thank you for your support. I feel fortunate to call you my brother! Harish Uthaman, you are the sweetest human! I can't tell you how much joy it brings me when I hear your voice notes. And I'll never forget the call you made after you read *Comeuppance*. I'll cherish it forever. Santhosh Prathap, thank you for all your kind words and support. Maanvi, thank you for being there.

Finally, I'd like to thank God for making this possible. Merci infiniment.

Bonus

Digital Pride is a series of LGBTQIA+ short stories written by Rathnakumar Raghunath that will be published every year in time for Pride Month. *Catch Me 'Cause I'm Falling* is the first story in that series released in 2021.

Catch Me 'Cause I'm Falling

Lately, everything kept making Abhi cry. He knew he screwed up big time getting suspended from college for showing up to class completely drunk. He couldn't help it. His parents were getting a divorce. Nothing was going to be normal anymore. If it weren't for this horrid piece of news that they'd sprung on him, he'd not have started drinking uncontrollably. He had known that they'd been having issues, but whose parents don't? ***All these problems usually have a way of sorting themselves out when it comes to parents. They should just suck it up and deal with the situation. They're not allowed to get separated. They're parents, for God's sake!*** Even as the thought crossed his mind, he could clearly see how ridiculous it was. His parents have always been supportive of him and the decisions he's made along the way. It's time he did the same for his mom and dad. They deserved happiness. If this divorce was going to give them that, then so be it. He has to make his peace with it. But this, however, was easier said than done.

All this drunken drama he'd been causing of late had put a lot of pressure on his relationship with his boyfriend of 2 years, Shray. They were the ones acting like a divorced couple. A few days ago, Shray told Abhi that it was over. All this out of character behavior that Abhi was displaying was too much for Shray to handle. It was like Abhi wasn't the man Shray had fallen for. It was over. They had broken up. They hadn't spoken to each other since. Absolutely no contact between the two. He knew he was in the wrong, but he never thought he deserved this big a punishment. The absence of Shray from his life was more than he could bear. It was strangely paradoxical that Shray was physically not present with him but was always on Abhi's mind. He was a permanent part of Abhi's psyche. Abhi couldn't stop thinking about him. Everything reminded him of this guy that he was so in love with. He wasn't questioning why all of this was happening to him. He knew the answer to that. He did it to himself. He saw it coming. But some naïve part of him had still believed that

Shray would stay with him through the thick and thin. ***Guess I was wrong...***

Abhi took his cell phone and looked at it. Shray was his wallpaper. ***What a stunner this idiot is! I mean, who looks that good?*** His long-sleeved Hilfiger t-shirt was hugging his body, accentuating his biceps even without his having to flex, making him look ten thousand times sexier. ***Man, those guns.*** He sighed and quickly went to his image gallery and made a picture of Michael Fassbender, his favorite actor, the wallpaper. He then went into his WhatsApp. The last text from Shray was from over a week ago. It was a reply to Abhi's text thanking Shray for bringing him back home safely the previous night after he had passed out drunk. It read: "That's fine. Goodnight. Take care." ***That did not even sound like Shray. It was so impersonal***, Abhi thought. ***He did not even say "That's fine, Abhi. Goodnight. Take care." He had never been that distant. He didn't even use one of those sweet names he calls me. How could he not?*** He was mad at Shray. He wanted to delete the message. But that was Shray's last message. He would regret deleting it later. He went to his gallery, to the folder named "Screenshots" where he had saved all the screenshots of Shray's texts that he thought were extra special. Abhi felt stupid, even a bit stalkerish for doing that, but rereading their conversations was one of his favorite things to do. ***If some guy did that with my texts, I'd probably call him a creep***. He opened one of Shray's messages. It read: "Hey, sexy. I still can't stop thinking about yesterday. You felt so good, Abhi. I'm getting turned on just thinking about your..." Abhi did not even have to force a smile. For a moment all of his anger vanished. He loved how Shray was the most gentlemanly of guys, but when it came to Abhi, he was naughty as hell. ***That guy sure knows how to make me blush.*** He went to read another text. "Abhi baby, I'm sorry about the argument today. I'm so sorry. I apologize for everything. I completely understand. Abhi, my love for you goes beyond what I can say. I don't think I can ever articulate just what you mean to me. You're all I think of. I can never stay mad at you. I love you that much. I always want you to be happy. Nothing in this world would give me more happiness than seeing you smile. I'm sorry again, sugarcane. And I need you to know something. You are the best thing that has ever happened to me." Abhi's eyes welled up again. ***He keeps saying he's not good with words. But he so is. He says just what I want to hear sometimes. But if I really am the best thing that has happened to him, why isn't he with me now? If my happiness mattered to him, why is he making me cry? Shray never meant those words! He's a liar. He doesn't love me at all!*** Even Abhi didn't believe that. He knew Shray meant every single word he had said to him. Abhi could never bring himself to hate Shray. That was impossible. Even though he was angry at him, he totally knew that he would melt if Shray were to come back to him. ***Abhi, why are you like that? You're stronger than this. Stop thinking of Shray. Get over him! He has moved on! Clearly! Why do you alone have to be sad?! You can't go on like this! Pull yourself together, man!***

"Abhishek, come down, kanna. Breakfast's ready. I made

your favorite red velvet waffles!" mom called out from the kitchen downstairs.

"I haven't taken a shower yet, Ma. I'll be there in 5 minutes." said Abhi as he decided he needed a diversion from thinking about Shray. His favorite breakfast could do just that. He went to choose what to wear for the day. He opened his closet and picked one of his favorite graphic t-shirts. "You look great in this tee, baby." He remembered Shray's compliment. He threw the T-shirt back into the closet and took out a plain grey one and a pair of jeans. Before shutting the closet door, he saw a paper cup with a Styrofoam lid, lying on top of a pile of his pants in the right corner. He took it out and admired it as if it were a prized possession. That was the coffee cup that Shray drank from during their first date. He remembered that day really well. He saw the scene in his mind, unspooling like a blurred film through the tears that were now filling his eyes. ***Shray's lips touched this cup. The same ones that passionately kissed me. The same ones that I'd never get to kiss anymore.*** Abhi felt like a bus hit him. Despair. He needed to snap out of it. ***Abhishek! What is wrong with you, da? Why are you acting like a child? What's with the cheesy lines? Dramatic much? Do you even hear yourself? Ugh...***

Just as he was proceeding to take a shower, his cell phone beeped. He received a text message. Abhi's heart skipped a beat. That could be Shray, wanting to get back together. He felt a sudden rush of adrenaline. He hurried to pick his phone up. He pressed 'open message.' The text read: "Abhi, I'm worried about you, da. I've not seen you in nearly a week. Is everything okay?" Abhi sighed. It was from his classmate Kevin. ***He has the heart to find out if I'm doing well but Shray doesn't!*** He immediately called Kevin to show his gratitude for the gesture that touched him.

"Hey, Kev! I'm okay. I've just been a little down lately. You know, with all the commotion that's happening due to the suspension and what not. But I'll be fine. Thank you so much for that message. I really appreciate that you care so much, da."

"No problem, Abhi! What are friends for, eh? Listen, maybe we could hang out some time so you can keep your mind off Shray."

"Whatever gave you the idea that I was thinking about Shray?!"

"Please, man, I know you better than you think I do! I know it's about Shray."

"Kev, you win! Anyway, I'll see you tomorrow. I'm starving, I'll go eat." Abhi hung up.

"Kanna, come down!" mom reminded him.

"I said, give me 5 minutes!" snapped Abhi.

Abhi sat on his bed, looking lost. ***Stop yelling at Ma! She's only trying to help. Abhi, you really need to get out. You've been completely disconnected from the outside***

world for a week now. But he had a feeling that he would be tempted to go see Shray if he went out. He did not want to reveal his weakness. He felt cheap that he was so desperate to want Shray in his life. He tried every way and means to avoid seeing him. He never left his house. He did not even listen to music because every love song reminded him of how it used to be between them. But all that Abhi was doing was cheating himself. None of this worked. Shray was on his mind, day, and night.

Is he thinking of me now? No, I don't think so. He's probably watching something on Netflix. He doesn't care how much I suffer. Why do I have to think of him all the time? Why can't I be like him? How come he doesn't have the urge to call or at least text me when I am dying to speak to him? Why can't I be heartless like him? He slapped himself in the face as tears came running down. ***Abhi, stop it! Stop feeling sorry for yourself. He doesn't deserve you. But you love him. Stop thinking about him. It's not worth it. But you've never loved anyone like you love him.*** He seemed to be contradicting himself. He felt like he was going to go mad. ***Is that what "madly in love" meant?*** Normally, the lame jokes in his head would ease the tension if not at least make him chuckle. But now, nope. Did not work. It only aggravated the entire situation. He was madly in love with a man that he thought would reciprocate his feelings at all times. But Shray did not. He was with him every single day for two years. They would spend time in college and go out in the evenings. On weekends, they would sleep over at each other's homes. ***Two beautiful years filled with love, and just because of a couple of rocky months in the recent***

past he disappears on me? How's this fair? He needed Shray's love. He was having withdrawal symptoms. He could not keep himself from crying.

He quickly ran into his bathroom, locked the door, opened the tap, and started to cry as the water gushed out from the shower nozzle. He cried silently. His mouth was open. But there was no sound coming from him. Tears streamed down his cheek. He wanted to scream. He did not want his mom to hear him. But he couldn't stop. He put his hands to his mouth. He screamed his heart out.

* * *

Abhi was standing in front of the mirror. His eyes were burning from all the crying. But it was good that he cried it all out during the shower. He did not feel like crying anymore. He dried his body with a towel.

"Abhishek! What's taking you so long? Come down!" mom shouted from the kitchen again.

"God, ma! I'm coming! I'll be right there." Abhi said as politely as he could.

He put on his clothes swiftly and headed downstairs.

"Hey, Abhi."

Abhi froze. He came down expecting waffles. Never even in his wildest dreams did he expect to see whom he was seeing.

After what seemed like an eternity, Abhi said,

"Hey, Shray."

♥

www.ingramcontent.com/pod-product-compliance
Lightning Source LLC
LaVergne TN
LVHW091304150826
845673LV00006B/1531

* 9 7 9 8 8 9 7 2 4 0 4 6 3 *